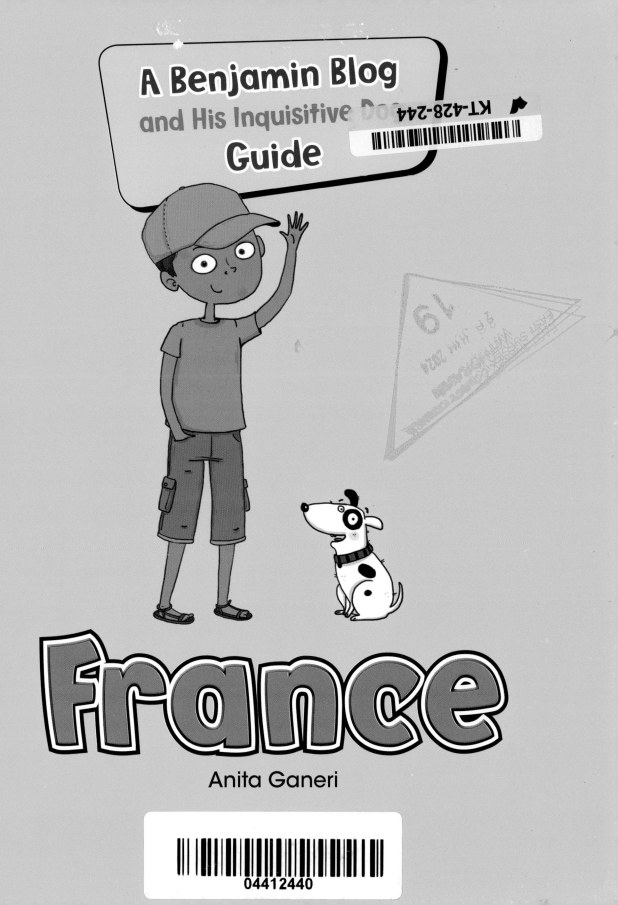

A Benjamin Blog and His Inquisitive Dog Guide

France

Anita Ganeri

Raintree is an imprint of Capstone Global Library Limited, a company incorporated in England and Wales having its registered office at 7 Pilgrim Street, London, EC4V 6LB – Registered company number: 6695582

www.raintreepublishers.co.uk
myorders@raintreepublishers.co.uk

Edited by Dan Nunn, Helen Cox Cannons, and Gina Kammer
Designed by Jo Hinton-Malivoire
Picture research by Ruth Blair and Hannah Taylor
Production by Helen McCreath
Originated by Capstone Global Library Ltd
Printed and bound in China

ISBN 978 1 406 28110 1 (hardback)
18 17 16 15 14
10 9 8 7 6 5 4 3 2 1

ISBN 978 1 406 28119 4 (paperback)
19 18 17 16 15
10 9 8 7 6 5 4 3 2 1

British Library Cataloguing in Publication Data
A full catalogue record for this book is available from the British Library.

Acknowledgements
We would like to thank the following for permission to reproduce photographs:

Alamy: Action Plus Sports Images, 22, Angelo Hornak, 12, Carlo Bollo, 15, Directphoto.org, 17, Jean-Yves Roure, 14, John Kellerman, 4, LatitudeStock, 23, Oleksii Sergieiev, 7; Getty Images: AFP/Lionel Bonaventure, 18, Bloomberg/Caroline Blumberg, 25, M G Therin Weise, 11, Sylvain Sonnet, 16, Visions of America/Joseph Sohm, 10; Shutterstock: Gurgen Bakhshetsyan, 13, Iakov Kalinin, cover, Kiev.Victor, 6, macumazahn, 8, Neirfy, 27, Paul Stringer, 28, PHB.cz/Richard Semik, 9, Prochasson Frederic, 21, WDG Photo, 26, 29; Superstock: age fotostock/J.D. Dallet, 24, Robert Harding Picture Library, 19, Tips Images/Dino Fracchia, 20

Every effort has been made to contact copyright holders of material reproduced in this book. Any omissions will be rectified in subsequent printings if notice is given to the publisher.

All the internet addresses (URLs) given in this book were valid at the time of going to press. However, due to the dynamic nature of the internet, some addresses may have changed, or sites may have changed or ceased to exist since publication. While the author and publisher regret any inconvenience this may cause readers, no responsibility for any such changes can be accepted by either the author or the publisher.

Contents

Welcome to France!

Hello! My name is Benjamin Blog and this is Barko Polo, my **inquisitive** dog. (He is named after ancient ace explorer, **Marco Polo**.) We have just got back from our latest adventure – exploring France. We put this book together from some of the blog posts we wrote on the way.

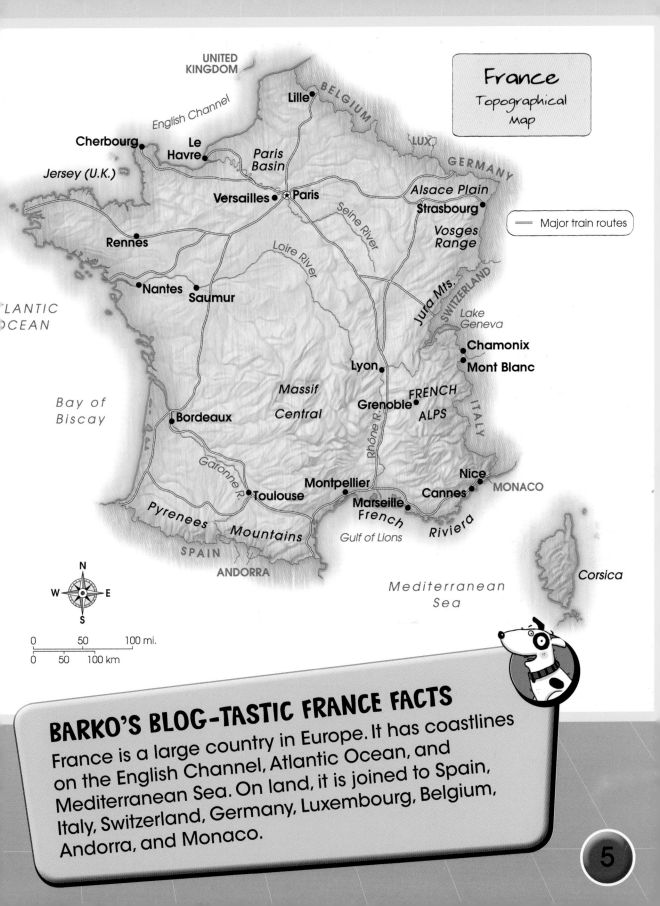

France
Topographical Map

UNITED KINGDOM

English Channel

Lille
BELGIUM
LUX.
GERMANY

Cherbourg
Le Havre
Paris Basin
Alsace Plain
Strasbourg

Jersey (U.K.)

Versailles ☆ Paris
Seine River
Vosges Range

Rennes
Loire River
Jura Mts.
SWITZERLAND
Lake Geneva

ATLANTIC OCEAN

Nantes
Saumur

Chamonix
Mont Blanc

Lyon

Massif Central

FRENCH ALPS

Bay of Biscay

Grenoble

Rhône R.

ITALY

Bordeaux

Garonne R.

Nice

Montpellier
Cannes
MONACO

Toulouse

Marseille
French Riviera

Pyrenees Mountains

Gulf of Lions

SPAIN

ANDORRA

Mediterranean Sea

Corsica

===== Major train routes

N
W   E
S

0   50   100 mi.
0   50   100 km

BARKO'S BLOG-TASTIC FRANCE FACTS

France is a large country in Europe. It has coastlines on the English Channel, Atlantic Ocean, and Mediterranean Sea. On land, it is joined to Spain, Italy, Switzerland, Germany, Luxembourg, Belgium, Andorra, and Monaco.

Palaces and statues

The first stop on our tour is the magnificent Palace of Versailles outside Paris. It was first built by King Louis XIII, who ruled France from 1643 to 1715. It was later changed into a palace by King Louis XIV. Now it has more than 2,000 rooms, so it is easy to get lost. I sent Barko off to find a guide.

BARKO'S BLOG-TASTIC FRANCE FACTS

Napoleon Bonaparte was a brilliant army general who made himself **emperor** of France in 1804. However, he was beaten by the British in 1815 at the Battle of Waterloo. No wonder this statue of Napoleon looks so cross!

Mountains, rivers, and beaches

Posted by: Ben Blog | 14 April at 7.56 a.m.

From Versailles, we headed to the Alps to climb Mont Blanc. It is the highest mountain in France at 4,807 metres (15,771 feet). If you do not like climbing, you can always go skiing or walking at the nearby town of Chamonix instead.

BARKO'S BLOG-TASTIC FRANCE FACTS

The Loire is the longest river in France. It flows for 1,020 kilometres (634 miles), from the Massif Central mountains to the Atlantic Ocean. It is famous for its **châteaux**, like this one at Saumur.

After a hard day's climbing, we needed a rest, so we travelled south for a little sunbathing. This stretch of coast is called the French Riviera, and it is famous for its sunny weather and sandy beaches. There are also beaches and sensational **sand dunes** along the west coast.

BARKO'S BLOG-TASTIC FRANCE FACTS

The Camargue is a huge **marsh** in the south of France, where the river Rhône flows into the sea. It is home to hundreds of birds, including pink flamingos, as well as herds of wild horses and bulls.

Big cities

Posted by: Ben Blog | 3 May at 11.49 a.m.

Our next stop was Paris, the capital city of France. It is famous for the Notre Dame Cathedral, the Arc de Triomphe, the Louvre museum, and lots more besides. The best way to get around is by the underground, which is known as the Métro. I just need to work out which train to catch!

BARKO'S BLOG-TASTIC FRANCE FACTS

Marseilles is France's second biggest city and its main **port**. Each year, millions of tonnes of goods, such as oil, chemicals, plastics, and olive oil, pass through the busy port.

Bonjour!

Posted by: Ben Blog | 5 May at 11.23 a.m.

While we are here, I am trying to learn some French. It is going quite well so far. *Bonjour* means "hello" and *au revoir* means "good-bye." "*Je m'appelle Benjamin Blog. C'est mon chien, Barko,*" means "My name is Benjamin Blog. This is my dog, Barko."

BARKO'S BLOG-TASTIC FRANCE FACTS

Some countries in Africa were once ruled by France. Many people from these countries have come to live in France. These women are wearing traditional African scarves and clothing.

In France, children have to go to school between the ages of 6 and 16. These children are at an *école* (primary school). When they are 11, they go to a *collège* (middle school). Then, at 15, they move on to a *lycée* (high school). Older children sometimes go to school on Saturday mornings too!

BARKO'S BLOG-TASTIC FRANCE FACTS

Many French people live in apartments in cities. Some apartment buildings, such as this one, are very old. In many cities, high-rise buildings and skyscrapers are not allowed.

Well, we are back in Paris for Bastille Day. It is a national holiday, and everyone is out celebrating. On 14 July 1789, an angry crowd attacked the Bastille prison in Paris. They were tired of being hungry and poor while the king lived in luxury. Afterward, France got rid of the king and became a **republic**.

BARKO'S BLOG-TASTIC FRANCE FACTS

Many French people are **Roman Catholics**. There are also many **Muslims**. Many come from countries in North Africa that were once ruled by France.

Lunchtime

Posted by: Ben Blog | 16 July at 1.15 p.m.

French food is famous all over the world, so we treated ourselves to lunch in a café. France is especially famous for its **pâté**, cooked meats, and cheese. People shop in supermarkets but also in local markets for fruit and vegetables.

BARKO'S BLOG-TASTIC FRANCE FACTS

I popped into this **boulangerie** to buy a loaf of bread. These long loaves are called **baguettes**. They are crispy on the outside and chewy inside. Delicious!

Taking a break

Posted by: Ben Blog | 28 July at 10.02 a.m.

Here in Provence, we are watching the Tour de France. It is one of the most popular sporting events in France. Around 200 cyclists take part in the race, which lasts for 23 days and covers about (3,200 kilometres (2,000 miles). The leader wears a yellow jersey – that's him now.

BARKO'S BLOG-TASTIC FRANCE FACTS

Boules is a game that is played all over France. The aim is to get your boule (ball) as close as possible to a smaller ball, called the cochonnet (jack). For some reason, the players get really annoyed if I run off with any of the balls!

From farms to factories

Posted by: Ben Blog | 2 August at 4.36 p.m.

These **vineyards** in Bordeaux grow grapes, which are made into wine. French wine is world famous, and about 8 billion bottles are produced each year. Farmers also grow fruit, wheat, olives, and sunflowers. They keep sheep, pigs, and chickens. Some raise cattle for their meat and milk.

AIRBUS

BARKO'S BLOG-TASTIC FRANCE FACTS

Thousands of French people work in high-tech factories. This factory in Toulouse builds the Airbus 380 – the world's largest aeroplane. French factories also produce around 131,000 cars every month.

And finally ...

Posted by: Ben Blog | 23 August at 9.55 a.m.

For the last stop on our trip, it was back to Paris. Here is a photo that Barko took of me in front of the amazing Eiffel Tower. It was built in **1889** from over **9,000** tonnes of steel. The tower is **324** metres (**1,063** feet) tall, and I am taking the lift to the third level for a breathtaking view of the city.

BARKO'S BLOG-TASTIC FRANCE FACTS

The beautiful **Château** of Chambord stands by the river Loire. It is around 500 years old. It is famous for its double, spiral staircase – one person can walk up and one person can walk down without meeting on the way.

France fact file

Area: 551,500 square kilometres
(212,935 square miles)

Population: 65,951,600 (2013)

Capital city: Paris

Other main cities: Marseilles; Lyon; Lille

Language: French

Main religion: Christianity (Roman Catholic)

Highest mountain: Mont Blanc
(4,807 metres/15,771 feet)

Longest river: Loire
(1,020 kilometres/634 miles)

Currency: Euro

France quiz

Find out how much you know about France with our quick quiz.

1. How do you say "hello" in French?
a) *au revoir*
b) *bonsoir*
c) *bonjour*

2. Which is the highest mountain in France?
a) Mont Blanc
b) Mount Everest
c) Mount Vesuvius

3. What is a **baguette**?
a) a loaf of bread
b) a type of sausage
c) a hat

4. What type of race is the Tour de France?
a) running
b) motor
c) cycling

5. What is this?

Glossary

baguette a long loaf of French bread

boulangerie a French word for a bakery

château a French castle, often found along the river Loire

emperor a ruler

inquisitive being interested in learning about the world

Marco Polo explorer who lived from about 1254 to 1324; he travelled from Italy to China

marsh flooded land, often around the edges of lakes

Muslim a person who follows the religion of Islam

pâté a paste made from meat

port a town or city next to a river or the sea, where ships load and unload goods

republic a country ruled by a president who is elected by the people

Roman Catholic a Christian who belongs to the Roman Catholic Church

sand dune a giant heap of sand, piled up by the wind

vineyard a place where grapes are grown for making into wine

Find out more

Books

France in Our World (Countries in Our World),
Camilla de la Bedoyere (Franklin Watts, 2013)

France (My Country), Annabelle Lynch
(Franklin Watts, 2012)

France (A World of Food), Kathy Elgin
(Franklin Watts, 2010)

Websites

kids.nationalgeographic.com/kids/places
The National Geographic website has lots of
information, photos, and maps of countries around
the world.

www.worldatlas.com
Packed with information about various countries,
this website includes flags, time zones, facts, maps,
and timelines.

Index